THE COM...

Plotting your course to Heaven

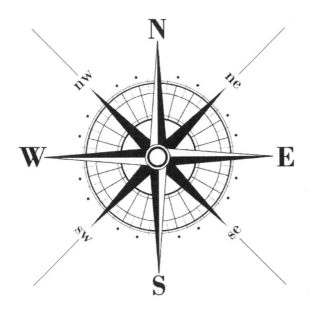

By: Michael Dugan

THE COMPASS

Plotting your course to Heaven

MATTHEW 5:14-16

"...like a city on a hilltop that cannot be hidden. No one lights a lamp and then puts it under a basket. Instead, a lamp is placed on a stand, where it gives light to everyone in the house. In the same way, let your good deeds shine out for all to see..." (4)

ISBN: 9781515082361

Available for sale through:

Dugan Data Inc.

800/949 252-0245, dugandata@earthlink.net

Amazon.com

Paperback and Kindle version

Special thanks to

Dr. Aaron Mansfield

Andrea Fingerson

Bruce McKay

Table of Contents

Chapter One   Introduction   5

Chapter Two   Base Plate   11

Chapter Three   North   19

Chapter Four   West   27

Chapter Five   East   39

Chapter Six   South   47

Chapter Seven   Conclusion   55

Chapter Eight   Let Your Journey Begin   61

Appendix   81

Chapter One

Introduction

Have you ever wondered how much God loves you? Have you ever wondered if he loves you at all? Well let me tell you a story about something that happened a long time ago in a distant land.

It was a Friday afternoon and God was walking towards the balcony of Heaven to see what all the commotion was about that had the angels in such an uproar. They made a path for him as he walked over to the balcony and looked down upon the earth. Michael came up behind him on his right and Gabriel stood behind him on his left. All the angels of Heaven pushed against them as they tried to push God out of the way, so they could swoop down on the earth and rescue Jesus.

"Let us go God. That is your son. Look at what they are doing to him!" Michael screamed in God's ear. "You commissioned us to watch over him and keep him safe and now look at what they are doing to him. I told him he should go as a king. He would have been more powerful than David. He could have ruled the world from Jerusalem and we would have conquered all the countries that dared to oppose him. We would have fought every fight, made war on anyone who opposed him and made all his enemies bow down before him so he could rule the world, because he is the Son of God."

"You have the power of Heaven at your command. Let us go and wipe those Romans off the face of this earth." Gabriel shouted as he pushed against God's arm and felt the forces of Heaven at his back, almost pushing him off the balcony. "The Roman Empire is so great? We could deliver you the city of Rome by night fall – just let us go, God!"

"I told him he should go and enjoy more riches and fame than Solomon. We could have gathered all the riches of the world and brought them to his feet. He would have so much fame and fortune there would not be a kingdom in the entire world that would dare to challenge him. They would all come to worship him and seek his wisdom, the wisdom of God. The multitudes that would come would be far greater than those which came to Solomon when he ruled before him."

The angels pounded their sickles into the floor of Heaven and the noise it made could be heard on earth like the thunder of a great storm. Their swords flashed with fire as they clashed together. On earth it appeared like lightning coming out of the sky. All of Heaven was a storm, a maddening array of fire, lightning and thunder as the angels screamed into God's ear to cut them loose and let them rescue Jesus from the hands of mankind.

That was the scene in Heaven as mankind beat, tortured, crucified and ultimately murdered the Son of God. And with all his strength God spread out his arms and held back all the forces of Heaven - and with a tear in his eye watched us murder his son.

I am not going to be so presumptuous to say that this is exactly what happened in Heaven on that Friday afternoon over 1900 years ago, but I do know God sacrificed his son for our sins, so that if we choose to accept him into our lives we could spend eternity with him in heaven. It is written in John 3:16 *"For God so loved the world that he gave his one and only son, that whoever believes in him shall not perish, but have eternal life,"* (2).

I know the question that immediately comes to mind is, if God loves us so much why is the world blowing up all around us and why are so many terrible things happening? The best answer I have for that question, I found in the Bible. In John 16:33 Jesus said, *"I have told you these things, so that in me you may have peace. In this world you will have trouble...,"* (2).

Jesus told us there will be pain in our lives and there will be no Heaven on earth, until God brings it to us. Revelation (the last book in the Bible) 21:2-4 states, *"I saw the Holy City, the New Jerusalem, coming down out of Heaven from God, prepared as a bride beautifully dressed for her husband. And I heard a loud voice from the throne saying, now the dwelling of God is with men, and he will live with them. They will be his people, and God himself will be with them and be their God. He will wipe every tear from their eyes. There will be no more death or mourning or crying or pain, for the old order of things has passed away,"* (2). You can see from these two passages that God is on the way, but until he gets here, we will have to live with the pain that life hands us.

My philosophy on life is pretty simple: you live and die and somewhere in between you find Jesus, you let him into your life and try to live your life in a way that is pleasing to the Lord, and when you die, you get to spend eternity with him in Heaven. So my journey's end is Heaven and my mission in life is to stay the course and keep my eye on the prize, which is eternity in Heaven.

When I look at life I see it as a journey. In early times people followed the sun, the moon and the stars. Then man created maps and compasses and used them to find his way. These are the tools we use to get to our desired destination.

So, like any journey, I need a map to show me the way and a compass to help me stay on course. The map I use is the Bible. It is the word of God, as we are told in II Timothy 3:16: *"All scripture is inspired by God and is useful to teach us what is true and to make us realize what is wrong in our lives. It corrects us when we are wrong and teaches us to do what is right,"* (4). It is his word that keeps me on the right path, helps me to avoid life's pitfalls and shows me the way to my destination. The Bible is also the source from which I built my compass, so when I get blown off course by life and all its demands and distractions I am able to take a new heading to get back on course and find my way.

In this book, I would like to show you how I built my compass, from the word of God, to help me to stay on the course I have chosen to follow. Oh, and by the way, I didn't choose that course. God chose it for me. I finally opened up my eyes and accepted him into my life. God has chosen the same course for you as well, and he hopes you will also accept him into your life. Believe me, he is looking forward to the day when you stand before him and he can say: "Welcome my son, welcome my daughter."

CHAPTER 2
The Base Plate, Joshua 1:8

"Study this Book of Instruction continually. Meditate on it day and night so you will be sure to obey everything written in it. Only then will you prosper and succeed in all you do." (4)

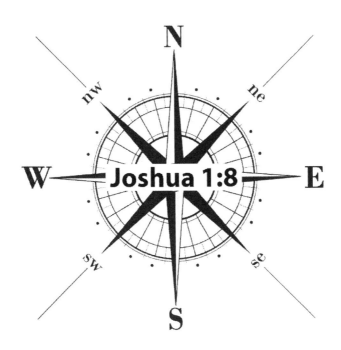

God told Joshua to do this the night before he took over for Moses (after his death). When I read this I thought, here is a prophet of God, a man chosen by him to take over and lead his people and God was telling Joshua to read his word both morning and night. I thought to myself, if God thought his prophet needed his word both morning and night, how much more do I need it?

We all know who Moses was, but how many of us know who Joshua was? Joshua was one of Moses most trusted disciples. Exodus 33:11 states, *"Inside the Tent of Meeting, the Lord would speak to Moses face to face, as one speaks to a friend. Afterward Moses would return to the camp, but the young man who assisted him, Joshua son of Nun, would remain behind in the Tent of Meeting."* (4). It doesn't say if God spoke to Joshua face to face the way he did to Moses, but he was in the same tent with God and Moses, and it seems that God welcomed him there.

When the Hebrews arrived at the Promised Land for the first time, Moses sent out a scouting party comprised of one leader from each of the 12 tribes. When the party returned only Joshua and Caleb had the faith to believe God would fight their battle and defeat the "giants" who lived there. The other ten men turned the people against Moses, which is why God sent them back into the wilderness for 40 years. From these two events in Joshua's life you can see that when it came to God, Joshua was all in.

The base of a compass is the foundation which supports all the other key elements you need to make it work. It holds the needle that points to the north and has the directions needed to guide you along your trip. It also supports the casing of the compass and the glass face plate which protects the integrity of the compass. I choose this verse as my base, because God felt he needed to tell Joshua this the night before he took over as the leader of the Hebrews and brought them into the Promised Land.

Another thing I noticed is that God did not put an expectation on this. He simply told Joshua to read his words. God did not say, read my bible in a year, or read at least 20 minutes twice a day. He left that open, so it would not become a chore which dragged on Joshua. No, he just said, read it! Both when you wake up and sometime before you go to bed. I think it is like many things in life, if we HAVE to do something it begins to drag on us. If we are encouraged to do something, we are drawn into it, and we do it more often and with a happy heart.

After reading this I started [to try] to read my bible twice a day. The morning is pretty easy because I get up about 5:00am and everyone else is still asleep. I can go down stairs, lie on the couch, enjoy my morning coffee with God, and after praying, pick up my Bible and start reading.

Night time is a little more challenging. By then I am distracted. I am trying to wrap up all of the "must dos" for the day and I still find time to enjoy my favorite TV shows. One advantage I have is that I teach Sunday school. By the end of the week I have to be prepared to teach the lesson. I alternate teaching the lesson with Bruce McKay every other week, but I need to be very diligent. The lessons are all based on Bible scripture so; I read them over and over all week long, along with the lesson so I am prepared for Sunday.

Using this method, takes me about 16 months to read the Bible from cover to cover. In all honesty, I probably read my Bible about 10 to 12 times a week. I seldom make it to 14, but I try.

What I like about the challenge from God is that, I can read as much or as little as I want. God didn't specify a length; he just said to read it. Every time I read it I find something new or I am reminded of something I forgot.

14

I find the Bible to be a very interesting book. If you look at it with an open mind, it is a history book full of many exciting adventure stories. It is also the story of God's chosen people and how, through Jesus Christ, we too can become his chosen people. In Ephesians 2:19-20 we are told, *"So now you Gentiles are no longer strangers and foreigners. You are citizens along with all of God's holy people. You are members of God's family. Together we are his house, built on the foundation of the apostles and the prophets. And the cornerstone is Christ Jesus himself,"* (4). The Bible is also an owner's manual, a guide to how we should live our lives. When you read about all the advice God gave to man, you realize that early man was pretty clueless and God was trying to help them out with his advice and his laws.

Once I finish, I start over again and by now I have probably read the Bible at least eight times. I have switched to different versions to add some variety. Right now, April, 2015, I am reading the King James Version. It is kind of fun because of the way they speak in this version. It is not that user friendly, but that is why I choose it this time. Bruce spoke about it a lot in our Bible study group, so I thought I would give it a try.

Another benefit I enjoy from following this advice is the time I get to spend with God each morning, before I start to read my Bible. When I first get up I have coffee and just enjoy my time with God. I lie on my couch, drink my coffee and enjoy the peace and quiet of being with my Father.

So, why do you think God wants us to stay in his word both morning and night? Maybe so we do not stray from him. A good example of this is Solomon. When he took over as the king of Israel, God came to him and asked Solomon what he could give him. Solomon asked for wisdom and knowledge to guide God's people. Since Solomon was so pure of heart, God granted him wisdom and knowledge and on top of that he gave Solomon wealth, riches and fame.

If we look at the end of Solomon's life we find a different relationship between the two. In 1 Kings 11:3-4 we find that Solomon, *"had 700 wives of royal birth and 300 concubines and in fact, they did turn his heart away from the Lord. In Solomon's old age, they turned his heart to worship other gods instead of being completely faithful to the Lord his God, as his father, David, had been,"* (4).

Maybe part of the reason Solomon turned away from God was because he stopped reading the word of God both morning and night and slowly fell away from God and his teachings.   One pattern I saw while reading the Old Testament was what really angered God was his people worshiping other gods. If you read Kings and Chronicles, you will see over and over again how the kings fell from power because they started to worship other gods or allowed other gods to be worshipped. If you are in God's word both morning and night, I doubt you will turn away from God and his teachings.

CHAPTER 3
NORTH, MATTHEW 6:33

"But seek ye first the kingdom of God, and his righteousness; and all these things shall be added unto you." (1)

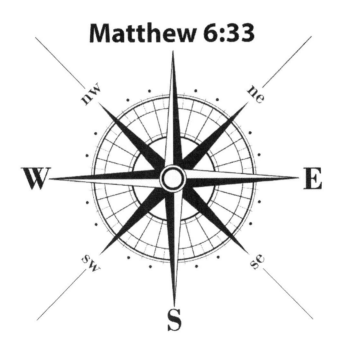

I think one of the best of examples of seeking God's kingdom first was young King Solomon. He was the kid born with the silver spoon in his mouth. He was the son of David, the greatest king Israel had ever known, one of the greatest kings known to the world and still remembered to this day. Solomon had a pure heart and truly put God before all others, and his only desire in life was to do a good job ruling God's people. Solomon got one wish, and he didn't make it about himself. He asked God to help him care for his people. God granted Solomon's wish and gave him so much more.

II Chronicles 1:7 – 11 tells us about the conversation God had with Solomon the night before he took over for David, as the new king of Israel. God appeared to Solomon and asked him what he could give him. Solomon asked God for wisdom and knowledge to rule over the people of God and judge them because there were so many. God's response to him in II Chronicles 1:12 was, *"Wisdom and knowledge is granted unto thee; and I will give thee riches, and wealth, and honor, such as none of the kings have had that have been before thee, neither shall there any after thee have the like,"* (1).

When I read this, I asked myself what I would do if God gave me one wish. I immediately thought – I would wish for money. I am 62 years old and I realize I need to figure out how to payoff all my debts in the next eight years so that I can retire.

God has already blessed me with a wife who loves me, three loving sons who are out of college and have careers and a house in the safest city in America (Irvine, CA). I have been blessed by being allowed to teach Sunday school for the past 15 years. But everyday I ask God to bless my hand at work because my finances are the area of my life which is lacking.

So, I started to picture what it would be like if I won the lottery and had enough money to pay off all my bills, and put enough away for retirement. I enjoyed the moment and imagined about how grand that would be but then something dark ruined the moment. A frightening possibility entered my mind: what if something happened to one of my kids, or to my wife?

If something did happen, I would naturally start praying to God asking him to fix things. I would remind him how he has blessed my life for all these years. He'd just blessed me financially and now a tragedy was striking my family. I would ask him; what is with that, God?

And what if his response was? "I granted you your wish, Michael. I gave you money. You did not mention your family or your health or your safety or any of the other gifts I have given you over these years. I gave you exactly what you asked for."

When I was done with my little day dream, I realized that God has lived up to his promise, he has given me all the great things in my life.

About eight years ago I woke up alone in Hawaii. It had been three months since my surgery and I was still lost trying to wrap my mind around the reality of what had happened to me. I remember lying in bed when this prayer popped into my head.

All that I am is because of you Father - all that I am not is because of me. All that I have is because of you Father - all that I lack is because of me. I will never trade you one thing you have given me - for one thing I have asked for. Because you are better at giving gifts - than I am at asking for things.

I realized in that moment that God had blessed me in so many ways and that I had never really asked for those blessings or acknowledged them. I was always too busy

22

looking at the problems in my life, that I could not change, and asking God to fix them. I was always too busy complaining and never opening my eyes to see all the blessings God had given me.

I realized how sacred God's gifts are to me. Regardless of what life throws at me, I am not willing to trade God one gift he has given me for one request I have made to him. I also realized that I am my own worst enemy and God is walking along side me, blessing my life in spite of myself. I felt relieved because I realized that God still loved me. He was looking out for me even thought I was lost. God was leading the way and blessing my life and I knew that in time, he would lead me out of this mess as well.

The things God has given to me are the things that are most important and dear to me. Not material items, but gifts that last a life time, blessings that can never be replaced: my family, my loved ones, my children. He has given them to me and he protects them for me. He does this not because of anything I have done. I just don't know why he does this and I don't need to know why. All I need to know is that *"all these things shall be added unto you"* are things he has given me, and I would never trade them for anything in the world.

I still complain to God, all the time, and pray that he gives me what I want and makes things better, but I always tell him, and remind myself, that I will not trade him one thing he has given me for one thing I am asking for. This is why I need a compass. I need to stay on course and keep God in my life everyday. I need to acknowledge that I am lost without him and that I need him in my life.

That is why I start everyday by thanking God for what he has given me and for keeping me safe through the night. I have always tried to be a grateful person and thank anyone and everyone who has ever given me a gift, so why not thank God as well. I realize he is God and he doesn't need my thanks, but he is also my Father and I am his son and I want him to know that I truly appreciate all the gifts he has given me.

So, every morning when I wake up, I say the same prayer to God. "Dear Father, thank you for giving me today, every day is a gift from you and I thank you. I thank you for my good night's sleep, I thank you for my health and I thank you for keeping my family safe." I go right down the list of everyone in my family and thank God that there were no calls in the night. I thank him that my family is safe and he looked over us and protected us through the night.

When I am done with my prayers and reading the Bible, I end with this same prayer, before I get up. "Dear Father, May you fill me with your Holy Spirit, bestow your grace upon me and pour your blessings over me. May you reach down and pick me up, yes Father, may I ride in your hand – in the hand of God. May you protect me from the evils of this world, which there are many, and protect me from the evil one who scurries about and help me keep my eye on the prize, which is eternity with you in heaven."

So, I guess I do seek him first. When I look at my life, I can see that God has blessed my life and he has *"added all these other things unto me"* as well.

So why do you think he told us to do this? I think he wants to bless us and to add good things to our lives. He wants to be part of our lives, mine and yours. He wants to have a personal relationship with you. I know I want to have that same relationship with him, because when I look at my life I can see that it is a good thing.

CHAPTER 4
WEST, MATTHEW 7:7

"Ask, and it will be given to you; seek and you will find; knock and the door will be opened to you." (2)

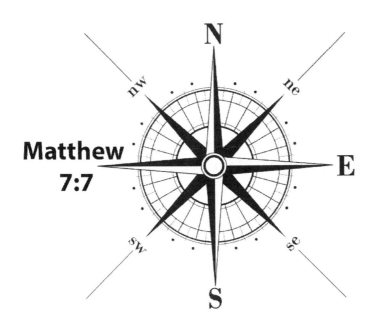

Jesus is welcoming you into his world. He is reassuring you that he is here for you and that all you need to do is come to him and receive his help, guidance and loving embrace.

ASK

I think "ask" is the hardest one for us to believe in, and the one where Jesus is really going out on a limb. I think all of us have asked for something from God and never received it. When we don't get what we asked for we may start to question; what good is he anyway?

My wife's sister was diagnosed with cancer when she was 38 years old. I am sure my wife asked and prayed to God everyday for him to cure her, but three and a half years later she died. So that was over 1200 times my wife prayed for God's intervention and her prayers went un-answered - what she asked for was not given to her.

Every night when I go to bed I say the exact same prayer. I ask God to please keep my oldest son and his family safe through the night, to bring my two younger sons home safely and keep them safe through the night, to keep Karen and I safe through the night and keep my mother and Karen's mother safe through the night. When I wake up in the morning I thank God for answering my prayers, because there were no calls in the night, he kept everyone safe.

Why some prayers are answered and some are not, I have no idea, but I have faith that God is there and hears them all. If you truly trust in God, then you will also trust his decision when it comes to answering your prayer. When Jesus was asked by the apostles how they should pray, he told them The Lords Prayer: Mathew 6:9-13. Part of that prayer states *"...your kingdom come your will be done on earth as it is in heaven...,"* (3). The part about *"your will be done"* is you turning your prayers over to God. You have to trust in and live with, his decision, his will. It can be a tough pill to swallow, but that is what faith in God is all about.

When my grandson was two months old the doctors told his parents he needed surgery. Since he was so tiny, they needed to wait until he was a little bigger before they could go in and do it. They told his parents, if it became critical they would perform it sooner, but for now they wanted to wait.

At Christmas Dinner when I said my prayer over our dinner table, I called out to God and specifically asked him to cure our tiny man. I even had his mother and father hold both their sons so God would know exactly who we were praying for. I reminded God that my son and his wife stood before him, that they affirmed their love for each other by being married with him as their witness. I reminded him how we had asked him to bless them with little Jasons and Jennys. Then I called him to look upon them and their two little boys and once again bless them, especially the tiny one.

I told God that my grandson was just a baby and that he needed his help. I was hoping that since it was Christmas and we were all praying for the little guy together, that God would miraculously come in the night and cure him. In my prayer I said, "We know that you can, we pray that you will."

Well in February the doctors took that tiny little boy out of his mother's and father's loving arms and took him into surgery while his parents sat there together with tears pouring down their faces and watched and waited for the doctors to bring their son back to them. At that moment God stepped down from the throne of Heaven, flew into CHOC Hospital, Orange, CA, took that little boy from his mother and held him in his arms while the doctors operated on him. When they were done, the doctor gave my grandson back to his mother and told her he would be all right. I have always believed that when you are in the hands of God, nothing bad can happen to you.

So, was our prayer answered on Christmas Day? No. But was our prayer ultimately answered? Yes. The human body breaks down and that is about all there is to it. Sometimes God heals it on the spot, some times God doesn't heal it at all, and the human body loses, and some times God just holds things together until we can get it fixed.

My wife still puts flowers on her sister's grave 20 years after her death, but she also baby sits her two grandsons every Tuesday and Wednesday. Yes, one of them will always carry a little scar below his tummy, but when she looks down on that little face, she sees that familiar smile she first saw 33 years ago when she looked down on our son. So, once again, she has been blessed with two bouncing baby boys to take care of, and thank God it is only two days a week!

SEEK

Life has many questions and, being human, we want answers. Sometimes we search our souls and find the answer on our own, but sometimes the question is so big and the decision will have such an impact on our life, that we seek other sources. Being the best father, God has given us his written word, the Bible, to help answer our questions and guide us through life.

Some of us seek answers to pretty things. Should I continue to date this boy, even if I don't see myself spending the rest of my life with him? Let's get real, when was the last time a guy asked his girlfriend to marry him and she told him, she would get back to him next Thursday. Should I take this new job offer in Utah, which includes a promotion, or should I stay in California with the people I know? Should I go to the Christian college or should I go to UCLA? These are all good questions, which could use a biblical answer and maybe some good parental advice as well, but what if your question is dark?

I came to a cross roads in life where I had to make a decision which was going to have a tremendous impact on myself and the people I loved. The decision was going to be so great that this is the only time I can remember, to this day, that I went to the Bible, to the word of God, to find his answer to my question.

This story is dark and my wife is probably going to kill me for including it in this book, but it happened to me. It happens to over 50% of all married couples in America. Like many married couples I came to the point in my marriage where I was ready to leave. Between 40-50% of marriages in the US end up in divorce (7). If you add to that the number of people who think about getting divorced and decide not to, I feel pretty comfortable using the word "many" to describe the number of marriages that hit the rocks.

By the time I got to this point in my marriage, I was going to church every Sunday and I had started to read the Bible. I thought if I could find God's answer to divorce in the Bible then I would know what to do and I would move on. I will admit, I was looking for the "Get Out Of Jail Free Card" answer, and not the "Man Up And Fix Things" answer. I started searching the Bible everyday, always on the lookout for the word divorce and what the Bible had to say about it.

Jesus thought divorce was a pretty important issue. He speaks about it quite a bit in the New Testament and The Bible mentions it in 68 verses (8). The verse in the New Testament that hit home for me was Matthew 19:8-9 when Jesus said, *"Moses permitted divorce only as a concession to your hard hearts, but it was not what God had originally intended. And I tell you this; whoever divorces his wife and marries someone else commits adultery – unless his wife has been unfaithful,"* (4).

Reading that verse pretty much ended my search for a way out. My wife never cheated on me, that wasn't the issue. The issue was my ego and how I thought she should treat me. I basically felt I should be receiving a lot more TLC from her then I was getting.

Let me tell you why I felt this way. We live in Irvine, California, which has been named the safest city in America many times. Irvine's public school system is so good; all three of our sons were accepted into University of California schools right out of high school. At that time in Orange County, 84% of families had two income earners. Karen, however, was a stay at home mom while Monday through Friday I was at my desk from 7:00am to 7:00pm and worked half days on Saturday. I was doing what 84% of my peers could not do and Karen was living her dream, staying home and raising her boys. I truly felt, that I deserved more attention and thanks than what she was giving me.

Well good thing for all of us, I sought the word of God. I try not to be a hypocrite, so once I got my answer, I realized divorce was not an option. With that decision made, I began to work on my self-righteous ego. I looked more at the fruits of Karen's labor and not my expectations of the "perfect" wife. Because of her we had a happy home and three very happy, well adjusted sons, running around the house. I don't regret my decision and to this day, I am glad I sought out the word of God. He answered me truthfully even though my motives were not so pure, but a bit dark.

Let me wrap up this story by telling you about the best date I've ever been on. It was our 25th wedding anniversary and Karen and I were in Hawaii. It was night time and we had our beach chairs and umbrella set up in front of the Royal Hawaiian Hotel on Waikiki beach. When it rained, I would put up the umbrella, when it stopped I would take it down. Since it had been raining on and off all day no one was coming down to the beach and I doubt ten people walked past us the entire night. We had the beach to ourselves; the hotel bar was serving up Mai Tais, and we heard the Hawaiian music in the background. I was smoking a Havana cigar and enjoyed the greatest time of my life with the woman I love.

Knock

So, what is this door? This is the door that opens up into God's world. Remember, God is a gentleman. He is not going to bully you into being his friend. He loves you so much he gave you a choice. You can accept him, or not.

He is inviting you into his world. All you have to do is knock and he will open the door and let you in. He loves you and wants to be part of your life. Like any loving father, God wants to show you the way to a happier and more fulfilling life. The only way he can do this is if you accept him into your life or you walk into his.

When I first started going back to church about 1988 there was an interim pastor at Voyagers named Wayne Anderson (9). One Day he said something very simple, that really hit home. He said, "Just come to church as you are, God will take care of the rest. How can he do his work if you don't show up?" Wayne Anderson was saying the doors are open come in. Just like Jesus is saying, *"knock and the door will be open."* It is that simple. You don't need to fill out an application to find a relationship with God, just knock and he will let you in.

So if you are wondering where this invisible door is, don't. Just knock. The door is right in front of you. Just put your hands together and say. "Dear God, please come into my life," and he will open his door and let you in. If you want a visible door try the door at a church. The nice thing about church is the guy up front has to do all the work. You can sit there and listen. We are all at different places when it comes to our journey with God, but I've found that a good place to start that journey is by walking into a church. For the most part those guys are pretty good and will bring you the word of God.

CHAPTER 5
EAST, REVELATION 3:20

"Behold, I stand at the door, and knock; if any man hear my voice, and open the door, I will come into him and will sup with him and he with me." (1)

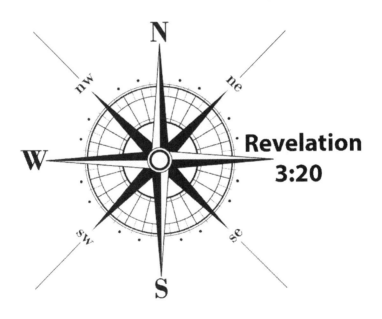

What another door? Yep, but this is the door to your soul! This is the door that opens up into your most sacred part, your inner sanctum, where very few are allowed to tread. God wants to fill your soul with his Holy Spirit, to be with you, because he can be trusted with your deepest darkest secrets and biggest and most fantastic dreams. He is your father and he does not want to judge you, but to guide you and be part of your life.

Do you ever get this empty, lonely feeling in your heart that just won't go away and you have no idea where it came from? Well that is your soul screaming out to God to fill it with his Holy Spirit. You may think this is a reach, but remember, we were all created in the image of God. God is made up of the blessed trinity (the Father, the Son and the Holy Spirit) and it is his Holy Spirit that your soul is looking for, God's got it and you need it.

When we were created by God, he gave us a soul. That is why we want to go to church and worship God and your dog doesn't. Your soul is super natural, it is what God put in all mankind so that we stay connected to him. When the soul is empty it calls out to God and it is you – the gate keeper – who needs to let him in to nourish it.

Think about it like your stomach. Does your stomach need food or do you? Let's say you get up late, jump in the shower and rush to work. Since you had no time for breakfast you grab a cup of coffee from the break room. Your boss comes in at 11:45am and tells you he needs a report done by 3:00pm. So, no lunch either. By 3:00pm your stomach is screaming because you haven't eaten all day and you need to. Just like your stomach can call out for food, so your soul can call out for God. You need to spend a little time with God to nourish your soul the same way you need to go to the sandwich shop and get something to eat.

So what is this *"sup"* he wants to have with you? God is not talking about having burgers with your co-workers at lunch. He is talking about a dinner that is followed by "I love you" or "you're the best friend I could ever have." It's an intimate dinner with someone who truly cares about you, a dinner where you share your warmest feelings and greatest fears. A dinner where you share your dreams and hope that the person you're with realizes that you want to share those dreams with them. That is what God wants to do with you and he keeps on knocking in hopes you will hear him and let him into your life.

My youngest son went away to college at the University of Santa Barbara. It was 149 miles from our house to the front gate. About twice a year I would send him an email and ask him how his schedule looked for me to come up and visit. We could go to dinner and then have a relaxing cigar on the beach and catch up.

He would usually get back to me within a few days and tell me next week would be better. He had a mid-term on Wednesday, but got out of class at 1:00pm on Thursday, so let's do it then. I would leave about noon to get through the LA traffic and would get up there about 4:00pm so we could go to dinner.

Right outside the campus gate is a little park on the beach. We would go there after dinner to have our cigars. As a little guy he used to watch his big brothers have cigars with dad so now it was his turn. He would always insist on me bringing "a good one," so I would bring a Davidoff 2000 or a Monte Cristo Court.

We would smoke our cigars, drink a couple of Gatorades and catch up on things. I would ask him how school was going, how he liked his classes and if he was enjoying his major. I just wanted to spend some time with him, in person, to make sure he was healthy, happy, enjoying life and preparing for his future. He is my son and I wanted to be with him for awhile so he could share his life with me.

He would tell me about all the classes he liked and the neat things he was learning. He was an Econ/Accounting major so he had a lot of teachers from the accounting world who would tell him stories about big business from the top looking down. The other half of his classes were pure economics taught by PhDs who wanted them to learn the theory behind everything. I could tell he was being exposed to both intricate economic theory and how it was accounted for.

He was enjoying it and the challenge was not an issue. It was fun and he was learning. Since he was living in a frat house I would always inquire as to how that was going. I wasn't real worried because he was getting good grades, so I knew his focus was on academia more than the parties.

At around 6:00pm, I would take him back to his place and head for home. So, what was my take away? I got to spend some time with my son and see how he was doing. By being there, I let him know I was there for him. Every time I left he always made a point of saying, "thank you, Dad, for coming up." What more could a father ask for?

What do you think his take away was? Probably, "Dad loves me, he took the time to come up here and spend the afternoon with me to see how I was doing." He knew I did not come up there to pry into his life, or try to direct things, I just wanted to be with him and share a few moments of his life. That is what I wanted him to know and that is probably one thing all fathers want their kids to know. I love you and I am here for you, always.

Since God created man in his image, then me caring for my son came from the DNA that God put in me. God is a better parent than I am, a 1000 times over, so he has the same feelings for me that I have for my son. He has those same feelings for you too. So he stands at your door and knocks, hoping you will open it and let him in. He wants to share that dinner with you. He is not there to lecture you, but to listen and help you to put all your concerns and dreams in their proper perspective. Not to judge, but to let you know that your Father loves you.

So, where is this door and how do you let God in? The door is your willingness to call out to God and let him come into your life. His presence is his Holy Spirit when he comes through that door and into your life. It is like that good feeing I get at times when I am at peace with everything. It is the feeling I get when I drive to church or when I get there, sit down in my favorite seat, put my hands together and say, "Thank you God, I am home."

I purposely put these two doors at opposing sides of the compass for a reason. I want to reinforce the fact that God wants to enter into your life. It is a two way street and either way he has given you a door to be with him. You can knock on his door or you can open your door. The difference between God and man is he will never stop knocking on your door. All you need to do is let him in. It is a door that opens into his world or a door that opens into your world – either way God is on the other side with open arms waiting to hug you and take you in his arms.

CHAPTER 6
SOUTH, JOHN 14:27

"Peace I leave with you; my peace I give you. I do not give to you as the world gives. Do not let your hearts be troubled, and do not be afraid." (3)

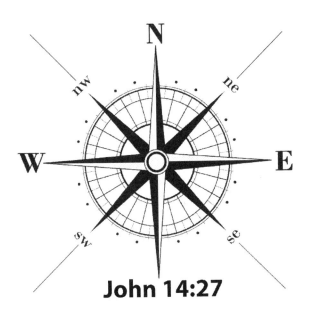

John 14:27

If there is anything I pray for now in my life it is peace. I am 62 years old and trying to figure out how I will be able to retire at 70. Quite frankly, I don't think it is going to happen. I can honestly say the first 62 years have pretty much kicked my butt.

When I was 53 years old I was swimming in our Home Owner's Association pool and got a severe case of heart burn. At first I thought nothing of it. I changed my heart burn medicine and a month latter got an endoscope to see why the new medicine wasn't working. After the endoscope the doctor told me I should look a little higher. I went to see a Cardiologist next and in the following 10 months I made six trips to Hoag Hospital in Newport Beach, CA. Four of them were over nights, and the last one resulted in a bypass surgery.

The nurses were always a bit puzzled about why I kept coming back. They never said anything negative, just a, "We will go in and have a look," but the look on their faces was always the same – you shouldn't be here. After all I was young and in good shape. I was swimming a mile every Monday, Wednesday and Friday and riding my bike 19.2 miles on Tuesday, Thursday and Saturday. I ate a cup of oatmeal every morning for breakfast and I did not put mayo on my wheat bread turkey sandwiches. I did not smoke, hardly drank and didn't take drugs or smoke pot, but here I was, back again to have more stents shoved into my heart or to take more nuclear treadmill tests which I seemed to beat most of the time.

If you are over 55 years old you've probably watched the TV show <u>The Six Million Dollar Man</u> with Lee Majors. Do you remember the start of the show? He would be on the treadmill, taking his high speed test run? That is what a nuclear treadmill is like, other than the fact that they shoot nuclear dye into your blood stream. Well, this was my fourth trip to Hoag and they decided to give me the treadmill test to see what was going on.

It was August, so I was pretty tan. I had on my shorts, running shoes and no shirt because they had 10 probes hooked up to my chest. It was really pretty cool. I was the athlete and there to race. I was ready to run, I was ready to beat that machine. You could hear all the beeps and watch every electrical wave length in my heart.

My wife was terrified because she had read up on heart disease and knew what was happening to me. I was in denial, trying to prove that this was not happening to me. When the doctor walked in, he looked at me and said, "What are you doing here?" Even the doctor was shocked to see me. I beat that test, but that was only trip number four.

The following February I took that same test and the party ended. 11 minutes and 15 seconds into the test my chest went poof. Four days later I was laying in the Cardiac Cath Lab at Hoag Hospital when my Cardiologist put his hand on my arm and gently said, "You're not going home today, Michael. You are going up stairs and we are going to bypass you."

When I left Cardiac Rehab two months after my by-pass surgery, the nurse brought over the final check list of life style changes which needed to be implemented for anyone with heart disease.

Stop smoking: I didn't smoke
Drink in moderation: I only drank from Thanksgiving to New Years
Don't take recreational drugs: I didn't
Get on a healthy diet: I ate oatmeal and turkey sandwiches
Exercise: She commented that my work out was harder than theirs
Avoid stress in your life: When she told me this, she looked up at me and the look in her eyes said, "You're screwed buddy." She knew I could do all the other things, I

had been doing them all along, but I obviously had very little control over the amount of stress in my life.

So how badly do I need the peace of Jesus Christ in my life? Desperately.

The stress of life crushed me when I was 54, but when I walked out of Cardiac Rehab it was right back into the same life. It was stress that put me there eight years ago and now I am living the same life and I have to make it through at least another eight years.

I find peace with God in a few different places. Every morning when I go down stairs and pray, I take time to just lay there and enjoy the peace of God. I just relax and enjoy the time with him. I also find peace with God when I ride my bike, which is now 16.6 miles.

When I start out on my bike ride I usually focus on the issues of the day. At some point, I realize I've been wasting time thinking about the woes of life, which I have very little control over. Once I realize this I start to focus on spending my time with God. I repeat John 14:27 and ask Jesus for his peace.

At some point a calm comes over me and I begin to enjoy my ride down the path. I look at my speedometer and see I am maintaining my normal speed. I check my heart monitor and see that my heart rate has dropped. At that point there is nothing I ask for, nothing I dream about having. I just want to enjoy the moment with God.

Easter week was last week and every Easter week I have my own little ritual I follow. On Thursday night I go to Maundy Thursday (this is a celebration of the Last Supper) at Voyagers (5). Then on Friday afternoon I go to Good Friday service at Mariners (6). On Saturday I go to Easter Service at Mariners, and on Sunday I go to Easter Service at Voyagers.

During this most recent Easter week I was laying on my couch one morning when I started to think about what Jesus went through on his last week. I thought about how he was mocked and beaten, how they drove the crown of thorns into his head and how they whipped him 40 times. I thought about the pain he must have endured as he was whipped so violently that his flesh was shredded from his body with each lash.

When I was done, I realized I was facing the back of the couch. I had pulled my arms up into my chest and my legs slightly into my stomach. Every muscle in my body was tense: I was scared. I had a physical reaction just thinking about the hell Jesus went through, just thinking about the pain he must have felt and the agony he endured.

I think we need to take the peace of Jesus Christ because he gave it to us. The price he paid for it was more painful and violent than anything I can imagine. He took all that abuse with out a whimper. He endured all that pain so that we could have peace in this world and the one to come. So, when he encourages us to take his peace he means it. He didn't go through all that hell for nothing. He did it for you. He did it for me. Take it and make it part of your life. He paid dearly for you to have peace and he wants you to enjoy it, because he knows how much you need it.

CHAPTER 7
CONCLUSION

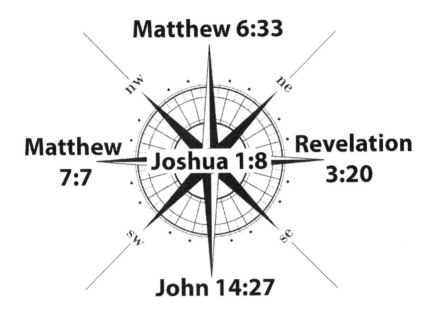

Matthew 6:33

Matthew 7:7

Joshua 1:8

Revelation 3:20

John 14:27

I believe in order to have a successful journey there are two things you must have: a map or a chart to show you the way and a compass to keep you on course. I have chosen the Bible as my map because my journey is to find eternity in Heaven with God. My compass is these few verses from the Bible which help me to stay on course when I get lost.

We need them both because we will always be blown off course. We will hit storms along the way and when that storm is over we need to be able to figure out where we are so that we can set a new course toward our final destination. Those storms that blow us off course are part of life. I get blown off course all the time. That is why I need God's map and my compass so I can set a new heading and find my way home.

Imagine you are on a jet heading from Los Angeles to Honolulu. The Captain comes on over the speaker and tells you he is going to change course and head south to try to get around the storm that is in front of you. Once he has gone 100 miles south do you think he still uses the same heading he used when he took off from Los Angeles? Of course not, he checks where he is, where Honolulu is and takes a new heading to get there.

It is no different in life, once we get off course; we need to plot a new course to get back on track. The destination is still the same, but now the direction we need to go has changed. This is why I have a compass and this is why I have chosen the verses I have. If I feel lost, I can quickly check my bearing to see if I am still on course. If not, I can make changes in my life to get back on track. I am human; I get distracted all the time and you probably do too.

You may wonder why I am so confident that I will get to heaven. The reason is that I have accepted the grace of God and I have accepted his son, Jesus Christ, as my Lord and Savior. It is nothing I have done. It is what God has done for me. When I accepted his grace, I wanted to know more about him so I started to read the Bible, his word. The more I read, the more I learned and more I realized just how much he loves me and wants to be with me. I learned that a lot of the Bible has advice in it about how to live my life and by following that advice I have found a happier life.

Have you ever gotten close to spending eternity somewhere other than this world? Well I have, it was a Tuesday afternoon at 4:00pm. Two nurses were left at the station and the waiting room was empty except for me and my wife. The only name left on the board was mine. After ten months of fighting heart stents, my arteries had caved in and I was going to have a heart bypass.

Right before they rolled me in, I remember looking up at Karen and saying, "Honey, tomorrow I am either going to see your face or the face of God. Either way I am going to be a happy person and you are going to have to deal with it. So I suggest after this is over you go home and get a good night's sleep." After that they took me in, turned off my heart, disconnected it from my body, hooked me up to a machine for four hours and started to reroute and replace the crumpled arteries in my heart. I guess my son thought the same thing, because he showed up about midnight and sent his mother home and stayed with me for a while.

I was ready to meet God, because I had accepted his grace and had accepted his son as my Lord and Savior. He knows I am a sinner and he knows how imperfect I am, but he loves me anyway. When he decides it is time to go, it will be time to go. So, on March 13, 2007, I got about as close to death as a person can get, short of getting run over by a cement truck, and I was ready to meet God.

Whenever my heart misbehaves and I get pains in my chest, I start praying like a mad man. This happens about three times a year and my heart gets lit up like a Roman candle. After a few hours of hell, I start taking my nitro pills in hopes of killing the pain. If it goes away it is a good thing, if the pain stays it is a bad thing. During this time I pray to God to help me, to save me and not take me. I guess when all is said and done, life is still very precious to me, but I know one day Karen won't be able to get me to Hoag on time and my heart will go click!

When that day comes I will stand before God with all my sin, with all my shame and with all my guilt. My head will be down, my eyes glued to the ground. I will be on one side of that great chasm, that separates man from God, and God will be on the other side. I will hear God call out my name from his throne. Jesus Christ will be standing at his right hand. God will have a book in his hand, The Book of Life, he will open it up and say, "Michael Dugan, let's see when you were..."

Then I will feel a hand on my shoulder and when I look over I will see Jesus Christ standing next to me. I will hear him say, "Father, meet my brother Michael. I died for him and dragged his sins through hell with me so that he could stand in front of you today and not be judged, because I have already paid for his sins. He accepted you as his God; the God of Abraham, Isaac and Jacob, the God of Israel and he accepted me as your son, as his Lord and

Savior. Remember, he is the one who used to ask us to make him perfect for just one hour every Sunday morning before he taught Sunday school."

Then God will smile, close that book, put his arms out and pull me across that great divide and say, "Come here buddy, give me a hug." With that, I will be in the arms of God and I will look up into his face and see all his glory for he will have given me a new body, a perfect body, for my new journey which I will be about to begin. I will have come to the end of my journey on earth and will be at the gates of Heaven. Then God will turn around, put me down and say, "Walk through those gates Michael, for Heaven awaits you, and now we can spend eternity together."

CHAPTER 8

LET YOUR JOURNEY BEGIN

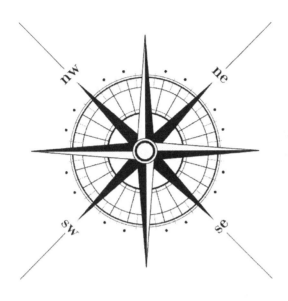

This time the compass is blank. This is your compass and it is time for you to find the things that will keep you on course during your journey. I feel pretty good about my journey and I feel that I have the instruments I need to guide me through life. They will keep me on course until my journey's end. So I've left you a blank compass so you can fill it in with the verses which have the greatest meaning to you, the verses that give you the most inspiration to create your own compass and find your way home.

There are 66 books in the bible, 1189 chapters and 31173 verses (10) to choose from. II Timothy 3:16 tells us that *"All scripture is inspired by God...,"* (4). We all know that sarcastic saying: "from God's lips to your ears." Well, in this case, these words were spoken from God's lips into the ears of his prophets, who wrote them down to create the Bible.

When we built a new chapel at Voyagers there was one Sunday when everyone got to take a Sharpie and write on the walls what God meant to them. The walls were still cement and the next day they were going to start dry walling over them. So, everyone got a chance to be part of the church, to write down what God meant to them, and have it sealed into the body of the church forever. As I walked around, I noticed the most commonly used verse was John 3:16: *"For God so loved the world that he gave his one and only son, that whoever believes in him shall not perish, but have eternal life,"* (3).

This is really a great verse and to many people at Voyagers that would probably be their face plate or their True North. It is a constant reminder of exactly how much God loves us. But now it is up to you. This is your compass, your tool to keep you on course. Maybe you have some favorites already and now you can arrange them in the order you want. There are four points on a compass, but there are also 360 degrees, so if you have more than five you don't have to choose between them. You can use them all.

I don't know where you are when it comes to your relationship with God. You could have none at all, or you could be just loving life and living in the word. We all find God somewhere in our lives and that is ok, because it is God's job to bring you to him.

Maybe you don't know God at all. That is understandable. If your parents never took you to church when you were little, how could you possibly know God? You were never introduced to him. My first two sons were about seven and four when we stated to take them to church. So, if you did not have a parent who suggested going to church, you could have easily grown up with out God.

If this is true for you, you now have the choice to find out who God is. As I told you, the easiest way to learn about God is to go to church. All you have to do is sit there and listen. Each week you'll hear a different sermon, another opportunity to learn about him. I went to church for about six years before I read the Bible for the first time. Going to church and listening to the sermon is a great way to learn about God.

Maybe you don't believe in God because of all the injustice in the world. Maybe you can't conceive of a Supreme Being who loves us while allowing all these terrible things to happen to his children. In John 16:33 Jesus told us, *"...In this world you will have trouble...,"* (2). In Revelation 21:2-4 we are told there will be no Heaven on Earth until God brings it down to us, *"I saw the Holy City, new Jerusalem coming down out of heaven from God...,"* (2). So like it or not, we are going to have to wait and there is nothing we can do about it.

Maybe you are mad at God. He did not answer your prayers or you feel he allowed something terrible to happen to you or someone you love. I think it is understandable to be angry with God and I have seen people turn away from him all the time. I can also tell you that I have seen the ones who turned away from him become more miserable over time.

If you are angry with God you should let him know it. If the only way you can tell him is by shouting then do it! He is waiting to hear from you. If the only way you can start speaking to him is from your pain then you should. He wants to hear from you and he will take you in any condition you are in. Don't forget, he watched us murder his son, so I am sure he can endure your wrath for a little while.

Maybe you put God on hold for a while. Maybe you were raised going to church and once you were old enough you stopped going. I was raised Catholic and I remember going to midnight mass with my sister and brother on December 24, 1969. The church was so crowded we had to stand in the hall way and listened to the sermon through the loud speaker in the ceiling. When the priest was done, we went home and the only thing I thought about was what a waste of time it was. I didn't think about the fact that I was there to celebrate the birth of Christ. My only thoughts were; I was done going to church and couldn't wait until morning to try out the new wet suit I had gotten for Christmas.

Don't get me wrong, I had nothing against God, I had just stopped going to church. I still believed in God, I still got down on my knees every night and said my prayers, but I stopped going. Just because I stopped going to church God never abandoned me, or stopped answering my prayers. Whenever my life turned upside down, I got on my knees and started praying to God to fix things. If something was really bad I would find a Catholic church, I guess I thought it was the only church God lived in, walk up to the altar, kneel down before Christ on the cross and pray to God to help me. And you know - even though I treated God like "911", he always answered my prayers. Never once did he ask me in a judgmental or sarcastic tone, "Where have you been Michael?"

Once I made a conscious decision to make God part of my life, my life got a lot better. I became a more loving husband and father. I became more comfortable around people. I also became more at peace with myself. I used to be at war with myself because I hated myself for all my short comings and failures. But most of all, now I realize that a crisis is not the end of my world, rather it is something I will get through with God at my side.

Maybe you don't have time for God right now. Maybe you are going to college and spend all your time studying and enhancing your social life. Maybe you are starting out in your career and your employer is taking advantage of you by working you to death and you just don't have time for church.

Maybe you get lost in life and have no idea why. This happens to me every now and then and did this past Christmas. I was going along loving life and then I got disoriented. I lost my zeal for life and for God. Sometimes life can be so overwhelming that I lose sight of the big picture and I get caught up in the day to day trials of life. I still pray, go to church and teach Sunday school, but I just feel lost, like when I went to Hawaii after my bypass surgery.

I get through these periods by going back to what I believe in. I look at my compass, look at my map and see where I am. Then I take a new heading to get back to the things that make me happy and bring me peace.

Maybe you are loving life and loving God. Hey good for you, that is how it should be. In that case stay the course, because you can see all the good it is doing you and the joy it is bringing into your life.

I'll bet you have one question and it probably goes something like this; does this guy really follow his own advice and does it work? Well, since Christmas (today is June 30), I have lost 21 pounds, started going back to Saturday night service and have written this book. You may wonder why I put in the remark about the 21 pounds. Well there are two places I find peace with God; in the morning in my family room and when I ride my bike in the afternoon.

Somewhere along my ride I always ask God to be with me. For the most part God shows up and I have a very peaceful and enjoyable ride. If he doesn't show up, it is because I am so focused on my problems I don't let him in. So, if you take 80 minute bike rides four times a week you are going to lose weight, and if you ask God to join you he will.

Every June on the last day of class with our sixth graders Bruce and I each take about twenty minutes to give them our farewell speech. Every year I put my compass on the board in hopes it will encourage them to stay the course and continue their walk with God. So I decided to take that little 20 minute lesson and turn it into this book to encourage you to find what I have found by letting God into my life.

I hope this book will help you create your own personal compass to guide you through life, to help you to stay the course and find eternity with your Father in Heaven. He has given you a map, his Bible, and he is waiting at the gates of Heaven to welcome you home.

YOUR BASE PLATE

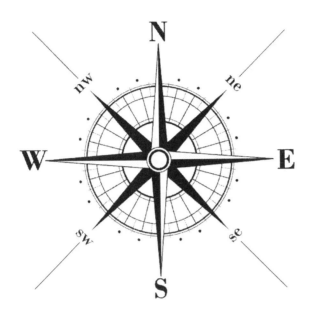

YOUR NORTH

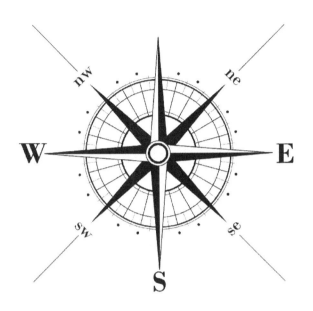

YOUR WEST

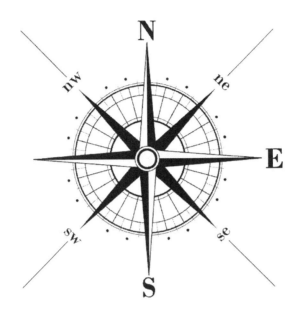

YOUR SOUTH

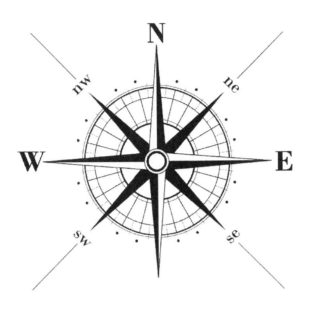

YOUR EAST

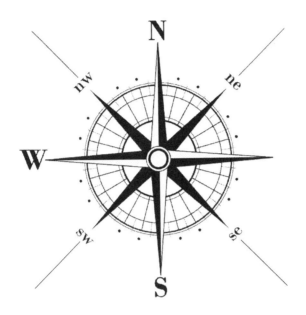

APPENDIX

(1) Holy Bible
King James Version
Omega Publishing House, Nashville, Tennessee
Copyright 1971, 1965, 1964 Royal Publishers, Inc.
Nashville Tennessee

(2) The NIV Study Bible, 10th Anniversary Edition
Zondervan Publishing House
Copyright 1995

(3) The Holy bible, New International Version
International Bible Society
Copyright 1973, 1978, 1984
Zondervan NIV Study Bible (Fully Revised)
Zondervan Publishing House
Copyright 1985, 1995, 2002

(4) Holy Bible
New Living Translation, Second Edition
Tyndale House Publishers, Inc.
October 2007

(5) Voyagers Bible Church

6000 Irvine Center Drive, Irvine, CA 92618, 949 857-5007

(6) Mariners Church

5001 Newport Coast Drive, Irvine, Ca 92603, 949 854-7600

(7) www.apa.org/topics/divorce

www.divorcestatisrics.org

(8) http://www.openbible.info/topics/divorce

(9) Wayne Anderson (deceased)

Centering Ministries, PO Box 9675, South Laguna, CA 92652

(10) About the Bible

www.christiananswers.net/bible/about.html

ABOUT THE AUTHOR

Michael's parents moved to California in 1966 when he was 14 years old. He has resided in Southern California ever since, other than for a brief period when he worked in Saudi Arabia. He received his Bachelor's degree in Accounting from San Diego State University. His first job was working as a cost accountant for Hughes Aircraft Company in El Segundo, CA. and since then he has worked for different companies in Orange County.

Michael is married, has three sons and for the past 28 years has lived in Irvine, CA. His hobbies were coaching his sons' soccer and little league teams, but now that they have grown up they include cycling and "light" weight lifting.

When Voyagers Bible Church put out a request for Sunday school teachers 15 years ago Michael wondered if he had the skills to teach children the word of God. He had been coaching his sons' soccer and baseball teams forever and thought - since coaching and teaching use the same principles, why not.

Not only did he have to learn the word of God in order to teach it, but he also learned that God wants us to apply his word to our lives. The lessons are not only about teaching the word of God, but also about teaching the practical application of them.

This is his second book where he takes the word of God and shows you how much God wants you to enjoy a happy and prosperous life. It is not just about reading God's word and knowing it, but also about applying it to your daily life so you can enjoy all the blessings God has waiting for you.

He can be contacted at dugandata@earthlink.net.